DRUNK DOGS

After last night, I feel doggone ruff!

CHARLIE ELLIS

summersdale

DRUNK DOGS

An Hachette UK Company
www.hachette.co.uk

Summersdale Publishers Ltd
Part of Octopus Publishing Group Limited
Carmelite House
50 Victoria Embankment
LONDON
EC4Y 0DZ
UK

www.summersdale.com

Printed and bound in China

ISBN: 978-1-80007-021-9

Substantial discounts on bulk quantities of Summersdale books are available to corporations, professional associations and other organizations. For details contact general enquiries: telephone: +44 (0) 1243 771107 or email: enquiries@summersdale.com.

DISCLAIMER: No animals were harmed or intoxicated in the making of this book.

I am off my furry face
and I am loving it.

WHICH IDIOT SCREWED
THIS CAP ON SO TIGHT?
I NEED THIS GIN INSIDE ME.

WAHHH! TOO MUCH TEQUILA!

I think I just sh*t myself.

NO, I HAVEN'T HAD
A DROP. HONEST.

Why oh why did I stay out for "just one more"? And Sharon needs these reports by noon. Bleurgh.

I don't have my ID, babe. You go up and get this round.

SSSHSHSH… PLEASE,
MY HEAD'S SPINNING!

SOMEONE'S SPIKED THE PUNCH!

Don't turn out the lights – the party's just getting started!

I don't know anything about how that mess got there. I was tucked up in bed all night. Honest.

Hey, get a pic of this, guys. I guess you could say my bark is worse than my bite. Hehehe. Get it? Guys?

Hey, is this the sun I just caught? Or am I wasted?

DID SOMEBODY
SAY SHOTS!!!

WINE TIME!

I SPILLED SOME SCHNAPPS
ON MY SCHNOUT?
THERE WE GO – ALL GONE.

Luckily the human is driving, so I can get *wrecked* on this road trip.

That feeling when you remember what you confessed last night...

Mmmm, that's just
what the dogter ordered:
the soft embrace
of hard liquor.

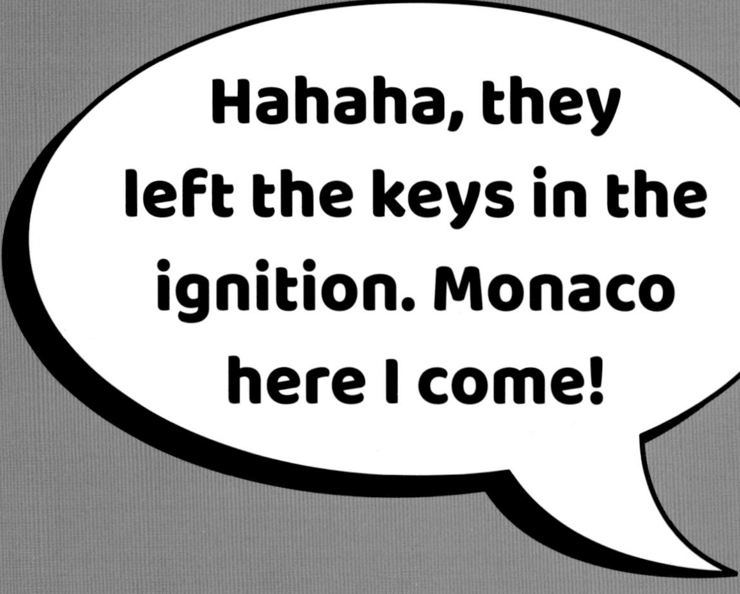
Hahaha, they left the keys in the ignition. Monaco here I come!

YES, I MUST BUY EVERY SINGLE CHEW TOY IN A LATE-NIGHT SHOPPING SPREE. I DEFINITELY WON'T REGRET THIS IN THE MORNING.

YETH, I'M QUITE THOBER, THANKS.

If I fetch you
this stick, can you
go fetch me a drink?

ONE MORE REFILL PLEASE!

Image credits

Have you enjoyed this book? If so, find us on Facebook at Summersdale Publishers, on Twitter at @Summersdale and on Instagram at @summersdalebooks and get in touch. We'd love to hear from you!

www.summersdale.com